ARTIFICIAL INTELL

COLLECTION

DATA GOVERNANCE WITH AI

VOLUME 2

AUDITING DATA MODELS

PRACTICES AND REGULATIONS

Prof. Marcão - Marcus Vinícius Pinto

Disclaimer:

Please note that the information contained in this document is for educational and entertainment purposes only. Every effort has been made to provide complete, accurate, up-to-date, and reliable information. No warranty of any kind is express or implied.

By reading this text, the reader agrees that under no circumstances are the authors liable for any losses, direct or indirect, incurred as a result of the use of the information contained in this book, including, but not limited to, errors, omissions, or inaccuracies.

ISBN: **9798344279343**

Publishing imprint: Independently published

Foreword

The explosion in the use of Artificial Intelligence (AI) in recent decades has profoundly transformed the world of business, science, and government operations.

At the heart of this revolution lies a valuable and often underestimated asset: data. More than ever, data is the fuel that powers AI, and how it's governed—from its collection and structuring to its auditing and application—will determine the success or failure of AI-powered initiatives.

This book, "Data Governance with AI – Volume 2: Auditing Data Models, Practices, and Regulations", is an essential work for all those who wish to navigate the universe of artificial intelligence in a solid and ethical way, with a special focus on data governance.

It is part of the collection "Artificial Intelligence: the Power of Data", which is for sale on Amazon and addresses a pressing question: how to ensure that the data used in AI is reliable, auditable and free of bias?

This volume is intended for a broad and diverse audience, ranging from professionals who work directly with data science and data engineering, to auditors, IT managers, and compliance and regulatory consultants.

Why this particular audience? Because for all of these professionals, a deep understanding of data governance isn't just a competitive differentiator — it's a crucial requirement for operating in an increasingly complex and dynamic regulatory landscape.

Data scientists and data engineers will find, in this book, a series of best practices and robust frameworks for creating and maintaining data models that meet standards of excellence.

Often, these professionals are focused on optimizing the performance of algorithms, but forget that the basis for reliable and ethical performance lies in the quality of the data that feeds them.

The correct structuring of a data model, the elimination of biases, and proper sanitation are discussed in depth here, offering a solid foundation for those who want to apply AI effectively and responsibly.

Auditors and IT governance managers can benefit immensely from the chapters that address the auditing of data models.

Auditing is the main tool to ensure that data models are not only functioning correctly, but also comply with regulatory requirements and are free of biases that could compromise their applicability in critical scenarios, such as financial decisions or medical diagnoses.

This book offers a detailed overview of audit trails, the necessary inputs, and practical examples, including an audit conducted at Google. For auditors, understanding the nuances of data governance and its intersection with AI is critical to ensuring compliance in highly regulated environments.

Consultants and compliance professionals will also find a valuable resource here. The international regulatory landscape is constantly evolving, with new standards rapidly emerging to address the challenges that AI poses to privacy and data protection.

The chapter on sectoral and regional regulations provides an accurate analysis of key global standards, from ISO 8000 to GDPR, as well as regulatory expectations from sectors such as healthcare, finance, and government.

For those dealing with compliance policies, this book offers a clear roadmap for navigating this complex terrain, helping to mitigate risk and ensure that AI is applied ethically and safely.

I hope that this book will be a valuable source of learning and that it will inspire you to apply the concepts discussed in your professional practices, always seeking to improve data governance and the ethical application of artificial intelligence.

Happy reading!
Good learning!

Prof. Marcão - Marcus Vinícius Pinto

Digital influencer specializing in soft skills for professional fulfillment of entrepreneurs, entrepreneurs, leaders and managers. Founder, CEO, teacher and pedagogical advisor at MVP Consult.

Summary

1	**INTRODUCTION.**	**13**
2	**PILLAR OF DATA GOVERNANCE: DATA MODELS.**	**17**
2.1	STRUCTURING A CORRECT DATA MODEL.	17
2.2	DATA SANITATION.	18
2.3	AVOIDING BIAS WITH WELL-STRUCTURED DATA MODELS.	19
2.4	IMPACT ON LLM TRAINING.	20
2.5	GUARANTEE OF SAFE RESULTS.	20
3	**AUDITING: THE MAIN TOOL FOR QUALITY ASSURANCE IN DATA GOVERNANCE.**	**22**
3.1	AUDITING OF DATA MODELS.	23
3.2	DATA MODEL AUDIT TRAIL.	24
4	**INPUTS: ARTIFACTS THAT MUST BE PRESENTED FOR DATA MODEL AUDITING?**	**27**
4.1	WHO SHOULD PARTICIPATE IN THE DATA MODEL AUDIT?	29
5	**DATA MODELING: GOOD PRACTICES, FUNCTIONAL AND NON-FUNCTIONAL REQUIREMENTS FOR EFFICIENT GOVERNANCE.**	**32**
5.1	BEST PRACTICES FOR DATA MODELS.	32
5.2	BEST PRACTICES FOR FUNCTIONAL REQUIREMENTS.	34
5.3	BEST PRACTICES FOR NON-FUNCTIONAL REQUIREMENTS.	37

6 BUSINESS RULES, VALIDATION, AND CALCULATION: STRUCTURING DATA GOVERNANCE WITH PRECISION AND CONSISTENCY   **41**

6.1 BUSINESS RULE.   **41**
6.2 VALIDATION RULE.   **44**
6.3 CALCULATION RULE.   **46**

7 DEADLINE CALCULATION TABLE FOR AUDITING DATA MODELS.   **48**

8 EXAMPLE OF A DATA MODEL AUDIT PERFORMED ON GOOGLE.   **49**

8.1 DATA MODEL AUDIT REPORT TEMPLATE.   **51**

9 REGULATORY INSTITUTIONS AND AUDITING OF DATA MODELS IN THE AGE OF ARTIFICIAL INTELLIGENCE.   **53**

9.1 GLOBAL DATA GOVERNANCE ORGANIZATIONS AND STANDARDS   **53**
9.2 SECTORAL AND REGIONAL REGULATIONS   **54**
9.3 THE ROLE OF CORPORATE INTERNAL POLICIES.   **56**

10 DATA GOVERNANCE AND DATA PROTECTION.   **58**

11 CONCLUSION.   **61**

12 FAQ.   **63**

13 BIBLIOGRAPHY.   **70**

14   ARTIFICIAL INTELLIGENCE COLLECTION: THE POWER OF DATA.   75

14.1   WHY STUDY THE ARTIFICIAL INTELLIGENCE AND THE POWER OF DATA COLLECTION?   75
14.2   WHO IS THE COLLECTION SUITABLE FOR?   75
14.3   THE INTELLECTUAL AND PRACTICAL VALUE OF THE COLLECTION.   76

15   THE BOOKS OF THE COLLECTION.   77

15.1   DATA, INFORMATION AND KNOWLEDGE.   77
15.2   DATA INTO GOLD: HOW TO TURN INFORMATION INTO WISDOM IN THE AGE OF AI.   77
15.3   CHALLENGES AND LIMITATIONS OF DATA IN AI.   77
15.4   HISTORICS ARE NOT A THING OF THE PAST.   78
15.5   CONTROLLED VOCABULARY.   78
15.6   DATA MANAGEMENT FOR AI.   78
15.7   INFORMATION ARCHITECTURE.   79
15.8   FUNDAMENTALS.   79
15.9   LARGE LANGUAGE MODELS – LLMS.   79
15.10   MACHINE LEARNING.   79
15.11   SYNTHETIC MINDS.   80
15.12   THE ISSUE OF COPYRIGHT.   80
15.13   QUESTIONS AND ANSWERS FROM BASICS TO COMPLEX – VOLUMES 1 TO 4.   80
15.14   GLOSSARY.   82
15.15   PROMPT ENGINEERING: VOLUMES 1 TO 6.   82
15.16   GUIDE TO BEING A PROMPT ENGINEER – VOLUMES 1 AND 2.   83
15.17   DATA GOVERNANCE.   84
15.18   ALGORITHM GOVERNANCE.   84
15.19   FROM IT TO AI: THE TRANSITION GUIDE.   84
15.20   INTELLIGENT LEADERSHIP WITH AI - TRANSFORM YOUR TEAM AND DRIVE RESULTS   85
15.21   IMPACTS AND TRANSFORMATIONS.   85

16   MEET THE AUTHOR. A RESEARCHER ALWAYS IN SEARCH OF KNOWLEDGE.   88

17   HOW TO CONTACT PROF. MARCÃO.   89

17.1   FOR LECTURES, TRAINING AND BUSINESS MENTORING.   89

17.2   PROF. MARCÃO ON LINKEDIN.   89

1   Introduction.

In the vast world of data governance, it is imperative to have a comprehensive and structured perspective to navigate the complexities and challenges inherent in this area.

In this text, we enter an unknown universe, diving headlong into fundamental concepts and practices that will reinvigorate the way we understand and manage data.

With an emphasis on the DAMA International Data Governance Framework, this work presents a sophisticated view of governance, data model auditing, abbreviations, and the histories of companies and institutions that have been consolidated through efficient information management over the centuries.

Striving for excellence in data governance transcends the immediate value that data can provide. We are confronted with the understanding that data is like crude oil, with no value on its own.

It is only through effective governance, careful analysis, and proper application of information architecture concepts that we can distill this crude oil into liquid gold, generating substantial value and positive impact on our organizations.

Inspired by the impactful words of Microsoft CEO Satya Nadella, we are driven to deeply question the role of data in our lives and the importance of governing it wisely.

Entering the chapters of this book, you will have access to a world of structured knowledge, where data governance stands as the foundation of efficient and sustainable management.

Through practical examples and theoretical background, you will understand how the fundamentals of governance are applied in practice and how we can effectively design structures to meet the needs of our organizations.

Auditing data models, an extremely relevant aspect of information management, plays a crucial role in our relentless search for reliability and quality.

In this book, we will explore the potential of this indispensable practice, discovering better ways to identify and correct failures, ensuring the integrity of information systems, and mitigating risks.

With a practical and detailed approach, we will learn how to apply the most advanced auditing techniques, which will play an essential role in our efforts to ensure the accuracy and security of our valuable data.

As we unravel the mysteries of organizations' abbreviations and histories, we are immersed in a journey through time, walking among the visionary steps of great leaders who shared a vision of the importance of data and left a lasting legacy.

Their stories will inspire us to raise our own standards, enhancing data governance and accelerating our pursuit of excellence.

As policies and standards present in this guide was developed based on the guidelines of the DAMA International Data Governance Framework1 and the DAMA Data Management Dictionary2, we have:

---

1 Data Management Body of Knowledge.

2 DAMA Dictionary of Data Management.

1. Definition of responsibilities.
2. Policies and Procedures.
3. Data quality.
4. Information security.
5. Regulatory compliance.
6. Definition of responsibilities.
7. Policies and Procedures.
8. Data quality.
9. Information security.
10. Regulatory compliance.
11. Metadata management.

Each body or entity in an organization's structure is a fundamental part of this data governance system and must be responsible for implementing the actions described in this guide, ensuring its success.

DAMA International's Data Governance Framework refers to a set of practices and guidelines established by DAMA International, a non-profit organization dedicated to data management and governance.

This framework aims to provide guidance for effective data governance within organizations.

DAMA International is widely recognized as one of the leading authorities on data governance in the world. Its framework is based on fundamental principles, best practices, and industry standards.

It addresses various dimensions of data governance, including strategy, organization, architecture, integration, quality, security, and compliance.

DAMA International's Data Governance Framework began to gain prominence as a world reference in the area of data governance from its creation, which took place in 1980 in the United States.

The widespread adoption and global recognition of DAMA International's framework is a result of its effectiveness and ability to provide practical guidance for implementing data governance.

By following DAMA International's Data Governance Framework, organizations can establish a systematic process to manage their data assets efficiently, ensuring quality, security, and compliance across the enterprise.

This involves defining clear roles and responsibilities, creating policies and guidelines, establishing quality control processes, among other essential practices.

It is possible to observe the Practices contained in the DAMA Model, as well as the practices adapted to the context of the Municipality of Belo Horizonte that gave rise to the institution's Data Governance Model.

2 Pillar of Data Governance: data models.

Building a correct data model is a key pillar for ensuring the quality and integrity of artificial intelligence (AI) products, especially in the context of language models such as Large Language Models (LLMs).

The accuracy, reliability, and impartiality of the data used in the training of these models are crucial elements for AI to produce robust, bias-free results that can be applied fairly and effectively in various areas.

2.1 Structuring a Correct Data Model.

A data model is an abstract representation of the organization and structure of data in a given context. It describes how data is stored, accessed, and manipulated.

When we talk about AI products, creating a solid data model implies a meticulous approach in defining how data will be collected, treated, and organized to ensure that the algorithms that use this data can make valid and generalizable inferences.

Among the main aspects that must be considered when creating a correct data model are:

1. Data integrity: It is essential to ensure that the data collected and organized in the model is complete and coherent. Missing or incorrect data can introduce noise into AI algorithms, hindering learning and compromising the validity of the results.

2. Semantic coherence: data must be consistent with each other and semantic and logically aligned to the application domain. Discrepancies between attribute meanings or data fields can lead the AI model to make erroneous interpretations, generating inaccurate results.

3. Faithful representation of reality: The data model needs to properly reflect the context it intends to simulate or represent. A poorly designed model can distort critical aspects of the domain, which results in skewed or limited learning of LLMs.

2.2   Data Sanitation.

A crucial step in the process of quality control of training data from LLMs, artificial intelligence products, and Data Governance is data sanitation.

Sanitation refers to the process of identifying and correcting errors, duplications, gaps, or inconsistencies present in the data set.

In the context of AI, it is essential that model training is performed with properly cleaned data to prevent the system from learning incorrect patterns or making invalid inferences.

Dirty or poorly structured data can result in:

1   Biased models: When the dataset has trends or patterns that do not adequately represent reality (such as gender, race, or class biases), LLMs can end up reproducing and amplifying these distortions.

   A classic example is gender bias in virtual assistants, which occurs when training uses texts that reinforce stereotypes.

2   Inconsistent inferences: Data with discrepancies or divergences from each other can generate models that are unable to make consistent inferences in different scenarios.

For example, if the definitions of a variable vary within the same data set, the LLM may be unable to determine the proper relationship between its attributes.

2.3   Avoiding Bias with Well-Structured Data Models.

Biases in AI are one of the biggest challenges faced today. They can come from a variety of sources, with the quality and structuring of data being the main ones.

Biases can emerge from the data collection process itself, from inadequate sampling, or from the use of historical data that carry discriminatory patterns.

A correct and well-designed data model acts as a first barrier against these problems, imposing strict criteria in the choice, treatment and organization of the data used.

How the Data Model Can Reduce Biases:

1   Representative Collection: ensure that the data collected is representative of the diversity of contexts in which the model will be applied.

    This prevents LLMs from being trained on data limited to a single perspective, which would result in biased predictions.

2   Data normalization and balancing: Data normalization—the process of standardization to eliminate unwarranted disparities— helps prevent certain subgroups from being overrepresented or underrepresented in model learning.

    Balanced data in terms of the distribution of demographic or socioeconomic attributes, for example, can reduce the chances of bias.

3   Continuous monitoring of biases: A proper data model also facilitates the implementation of continuous monitoring techniques, such as audits and post-deployment assessments, to ensure that the LLM continues to generate neutral and fair responses, even when confronted with new data.

2.4   Impact on LLM Training.

A properly structured data model not only reduces biases and discrepancies, but also optimizes the training process of Large Language Models.

When data is clean, complete, and well-structured, the AI algorithm is able to extract patterns with greater accuracy, allowing for deeper and more generalizable learning.

1   Reduced redundancy and noise: When working with clean, deduplicated data, LLMs don't waste computational cycles dealing with redundant or incoherent information, focusing their processing power on detecting useful and relevant patterns.

2   Computational efficiency: A well-designed data model ensures that processing resources are utilized efficiently, optimizing both the time and cost of training.

This is especially important in large LLM implementations, which require vast amounts of data and significant computational power.

3   Ease of adaptation: A good data model is flexible and extensible, which allows for updates and adjustments as new data becomes available or as the needs of the system change.

Thus, LLMs can be continuously trained and refined with new data without compromising the integrity of previous results.

2.5   Guarantee of safe results.

Therefore, creating a correct data model enhances the governance of the model itself and the governance of its data. Crucial aspects for ensuring the quality of artificial intelligence products.

Governance provides a solid foundation for LLM learning to take place in an efficient, bias-free, and discrepancies-free manner.

By ensuring that data is properly structured, sanitized, and faithfully represents reality, it is possible not only to increase the accuracy of AI models, but also to ensure that systems are fair and impartial in their responses and decisions, contributing to a more ethical and reliable AI.

As data scientist Cathy O'Neil put it in her book Weapons of Math Destruction: "Algorithms are opinions embedded in code." For these algorithms to reflect fair opinions, we must start at the base—and that foundation is the data model.

3 Auditing: the main tool for quality assurance in Data Governance.

Auditing is the process of systematically and independently evaluating an organization's activities, processes, systems, and information to verify that they are in compliance with established standards, regulations, policies, and practices.

The purpose of auditing is to provide an unbiased and objective assessment of the effectiveness, efficiency, safety, and compliance of an organization's operations.

The audit is conducted by qualified and independent professionals, known as auditors, who are responsible for conducting a detailed and critical analysis of the various aspects of the organization, with the aim of identifying failures, risks, opportunities for improvement and ensuring compliance with established standards and requirements.

There are different types of auditing that can be applied in different areas and sectors, such as financial auditing, compliance auditing, operational auditing, quality auditing, among others.

Each type of audit has its own objectives, scope, and specific methods of work.

When conducting an audit, the auditor utilizes appropriate techniques and tools, such as interviews, document review, data analysis, testing, and sampling, to gather evidence and gain a comprehensive understanding of the activities and processes at hand.

Based on the audit findings, recommendations for improvements are made and audit reports are prepared to communicate the results to managers and relevant stakeholders.

Auditing plays a key role in ensuring the transparency, integrity, corporate governance, and compliance of organizations.

It helps to identify and correct deficiencies, mitigate risks, improve operational efficiency, and strengthen stakeholder trust in the organization.

3.1   Auditing of data models.

Data model auditing is a specific process, within the area of Information Technology auditing, that focuses on the evaluation and analysis of the data model used by an organization.

The purpose of the data model audit is to ensure that the data model is correct, complete, coherent, in accordance with the best practices and established requirements.

During data model auditing, auditors examine the various elements of the model, including entities, attributes, relationships, constraints, and other related structures. They verify that the model meets quality and compliance standards, that it is aligned with the needs and goals of the organization, and that it adequately supports business processes and decision-making.

Auditors also review documentation related to the data model, such as diagrams, specifications, data dictionaries, and data governance policies. They verify that the documentation is up-to-date, clear, accurate, and covers all the information necessary to understand and use the data model properly.

During the data model auditing process, tests and validations can be performed to ensure the integrity and quality of the data stored in the model.

Auditors can also assess the security, performance, and scalability of the model, as well as its ability to withstand future requirements and changes in the technological environment.

At the end of the data model audit, a report is generated that describes the findings, recommendations, and conclusions of the audit. This report serves as a basis for implementing improvements to the data model, correcting potential issues, and improving data governance in the organization.

Data model auditing plays an essential role in ensuring the quality, reliability, and effectiveness of the data model used by an organization.

It helps identify areas for improvement, mitigate risk, and ensure that the data model is a solid foundation for the organization's efficient and effective storage, access, and use of data.

3.2   Data model audit trail.

The data model audit trail is a detailed record of the steps and decisions taken during the process of creating and maintaining data models.

Here's an example of a data model audit trail that you can tailor to context-specific needs:

1. Model objectives: Document the specific objectives of the data model, including the purpose, desired metrics, and goals to be achieved.

2. Data source: Identify the data sources used in the model. Record details such as the source of the data, the format in which it was provided, and any transformations or manipulations performed.

3. Data cleansing and preprocessing: Record the cleansing and preprocessing steps applied to the data, such as removing missing data, handling outliers, and normalizing variables.

4. Variable selection: Document the variables selected for inclusion in the model and the reasons for their choice. This can include exploratory analyses, assessing the importance of variables, and resource selection techniques.

5. Techniques and algorithms used: describe the modeling techniques and algorithms used, such as linear regression, decision trees, neural networks, among others. Also record the specific parameters and settings applied.

6. Model training and validation: Record the model training steps, including splitting the data into training and validation sets, as well as any cross-validation or hyperparameter tuning techniques used.

7. Evaluation metrics: Document the metrics used to evaluate the quality and performance of the model, such as accuracy, recall, f1-score, area under the ROC curve, and more. Also include the results obtained in each metric.

8. Iterations and adjustments: Record the iterations made in the modeling process, including any adjustments made based on the analysis of the results. This may involve trying different techniques, parameters, or approaches to improve the performance of the model.

9. Decision documentation: Take notes of key decisions made during the modeling process, such as deleting variables, choosing

algorithms, or setting parameters. This will help to understand the reasons behind these decisions and facilitate future revisions or updates to the model.

10. Versioning and change tracking: Keep a record of model versions, indicating any changes made over time. This will ensure traceability and allow you to follow the evolution of the model.

It is important to tailor this audit trail according to your organization's specific requirements and processes. Also, be sure to keep this trail up to date as the data model evolves and undergoes revisions.

4 Inputs: artifacts that must be presented for data model auditing?

During a data model audit, the following artifacts are typically presented for review and evaluation:

1. Model documentation. Includes complete documentation of the data model, describing its structure, entity relationships, attributes, data types, constraints, and applicable business rules. The documentation should also explain the rationale behind the modeling decisions, highlighting the choices made during the process.

2. Data model diagrams: Diagrams provide a visualization of the data model, showing the tables, relationships, primary and foreign keys, as well as other relevant entities. Clear and well-organized diagrams make it easy to understand the model and identify potential issues or improvements.

3. Data dictionary: A data dictionary is a detailed list of all terms, definitions, and descriptions related to the entities and attributes of the data model. It provides a complete reference for the elements of the model and helps to ensure a consistent understanding of the data.

4. Database creation and modification scripts: These scripts contain the SQL statements to create or modify the database's tables, columns, constraints, and relationships based on the data model. Scripts should be reviewed to ensure that they are correct and consistent with the documented model.

5. Data examples: Presenting real or fictional data examples can help illustrate how the data model is applied in practice. This can include data samples in tabular format or complete records to show how the data is stored and related in the database.

6. Validation reports and tests: Validation reports and tests performed on the data model are important to prove its accuracy and effectiveness. This can include results from health tests, performance tests, load tests, or other verification and validation activities.

7. Analysis results and metrics: If the data model was used to perform analysis or generate metrics, it is important to present the results obtained. This can include analysis reports, data visualizations, or graphs that demonstrate the information extracted from the model.

8. Change log and version history: It is important to keep a record of the changes made to the data model over time, including a list of versions and a description of the modifications made. This helps track the evolution of the model and provides transparency regarding the changes made.

9. Functional requirements: Functional requirements are detailed descriptions of the functionalities or behaviors that a system, product, or service must perform to meet the needs, expectations, and goals of users.

   These requirements define the specific actions that the system must perform, such as user interactions, calculations, processes, validations, and other functional tasks necessary for the system to achieve its goals.

   Functional requirements must be clear, measurable and verifiable in order to ensure that the system is developed and implemented correctly.

   They are essential in the software development process and systems engineering projects, as they guide the design, implementation, testing, and validation of the system, ensuring that it accurately meets the needs and expectations of users.

10. Non-functional requirements: These are specifications that describe the functions, operations, or actions that a system, software, product, or service must be capable of performing.

    In other words, they are the resources and behaviors that the system needs to have to meet the user's needs, meet the project's objectives, and ensure its effective operation.

    Non-functional requirements typically include information about how the system should behave in different situations, what operations it should perform, what interactions are expected from users, and what outputs should be generated in response to certain inputs.

    They are essential for software development and for ensuring that the final product meets customer expectations and requirements.

These artifacts provide a comprehensive view of the data model, its characteristics, creation processes, and changes made over time. They are essential for reviewing and auditing the model, ensuring its integrity, quality, and compliance with the organization's requirements.

4.1   Who should participate in the data model audit?

Auditing a data model is a critical process that must involve the participation of multiple stakeholders to ensure its effectiveness and compliance with the organization's needs.

Here are some of the key players involved in data model auditing:

1   Data development team: The professionals responsible for creating and developing the data model should be involved in validation. This includes data analysts, data scientists, data engineers, and other data experts who have technical expertise and experience in data modeling.

2   Business analysts: Business analysts play a key role in data model validation, as they are responsible for understanding the requirements and needs of the business.

They should review and validate the data model to ensure that it meets the goals and expectations of the business, as well as verify that the modeled data is relevant to the desired analysis and reporting.

3   Business stakeholders: In addition to business analysts, other stakeholders in the business should also participate in validation. This can include department managers, executives, domain experts, and end users.

These people bring additional perspectives and can provide valuable insights into the specific requirements of the business and the needs of users.

4   Data governance team: The data governance team, which is responsible for defining and implementing data policies and guidelines in the organization, should be involved in validating the data model.

They can assess whether the model complies with data governance policies, such as naming standards, data privacy, and security.

5   Technical experts: In some cases, it may be necessary to involve additional technical experts, such as database administrators, data architects, or information security specialists.

These professionals can review the data model from a technical point of view, evaluating the structure, performance, and security of the proposed model.

6   Internal or external auditors: In organizations that follow strict compliance practices or that are subject to specific regulations, the participation of internal or external auditors may be required to ensure data model compliance.

They can assess whether the model meets regulatory requirements and data governance best practices.

It is important to involve a variety of stakeholders to ensure that different perspectives are considered during data model validation. This helps to identify potential issues, ensure the quality and usefulness of the model, and increase acceptance and adoption by end users.

5 Data modeling: good practices, functional and non-functional requirements for efficient governance.

5.1 Best practices for data models.

There are several best practices for creating and managing data models.

Here are some of them:

1. Understand the business requirements: Before starting data modeling, it is essential to understand the requirements and needs of the business. This involves collaborating with stakeholders and clearly defining the objectives of the data model.

2. Normalization: Normalization is an important principle for designing efficient database structures. This involves splitting data into distinct tables to avoid redundancy and inconsistency, following normal forms, such as the third normal form (3nf).

3. Choosing proper primary keys: Correctly identifying the primary keys of the tables is crucial. A unique, stable primary key should be selected for each table, preferably using a unique identifier such as a sequential key or a uuid.

4. Clear relationships: Relationships between tables should be established clearly and appropriately. This includes defining foreign keys to connect the tables and maintain referential integrity. The type of relationship (one to one, one to many, many to many) must be determined correctly.

5. Consistent use of naming: It's important to adopt consistent naming for data model objects, such as tables, columns, keys, and relationships. This makes it easier to understand and maintain the

model. Naming standards must be defined and followed to ensure consistency.

6. Proper documentation: Documenting the data model comprehensively is essential. This includes creating clear diagrams, describing objects and their properties, associated business rules, and any other relevant information. Documentation helps ensure proper understanding and use of the model.

7. Flexibility for future changes: The data model should be designed with flexibility to accommodate change and evolution. This involves anticipating future requirements and creating an adaptable framework, allowing for the addition or removal of attributes and relationships without significant impact.

8. Validation and testing: Performing validation and testing of the data model is critical. This includes checking the consistency of the model, running queries, and validating the results. Performance testing can also be performed to ensure that the model meets the requirements for response time and scalability.

9. Data governance: Implementing data governance practices helps ensure data compliance, quality, and consistency. This includes establishing policies, processes, and responsibilities to manage the data lifecycle, security, privacy, and compliance with applicable regulations.

10. Collaboration and documentation of changes: Changes made to the data model must be properly documented. It is important to keep a record of the changes made, including the date, description, and justification. Additionally, it is recommended to involve relevant stakeholders in discussions and decisions on changes to the model.

These are just a few of the best practices for data models. It is important to adapt these practices to the specific needs and contexts of the organization, always seeking to ensure the efficiency, quality, and integrity of the data.

5.2   Best practices for functional requirements.

Best practices for functional requirements aim to ensure that the requirements of an information technology product are well-defined, understandable, and meet the needs of the end user.

Here are some of the best practices for crafting functional requirements:

1. Proper requirements elicitation: Conduct thorough and accurate requirements gathering, involving all relevant stakeholders.

   Utilize elicitation techniques, such as interviews, workshops, questionnaires, and observation, to identify and understand users' needs and expectations.

2. Clear specification: Write requirements in a clear, concise, and understandable way. Use simple language and avoid ambiguity. The requirements should be easily interpreted and understood by everyone involved in the project.

3. Identification of essential requirements: Prioritize the most important and essential requirements for the system. Identify the crucial functionalities that meet key user needs and ensure value delivery. This helps to avoid over-requirements and concentration on the most critical aspects.

4. Proper documentation: Document requirements in an organized and accessible way. Use standardized formats, such as lists, tables, or diagrams, to record requirements. Maintain

a clear and traceable structure for easy reference and subsequent maintenance.

5. Specifying testable requirements: Make sure that the requirements are measurable and testable. This means that they must be formulated in such a way that it is possible to verify whether they have been met or not. The requirements must be verifiable through testing or other appropriate methods.

6. Ongoing validation: Validate requirements with stakeholders to ensure they are correct, complete, and adequate. Conduct regular reviews and reviews with end-users and other stakeholders to gather feedback and make necessary adjustments.

7. Change management: Establish an effective change management process for handling changes in requirements. Record, evaluate, and track requirements changes in a systematic way, to avoid inconsistencies and ensure traceability.

8. Effective communication: Establish clear and effective communication with stakeholders throughout the requirements drafting process. Keep communication channels open, promote dialogue, and seek alignment among all involved.

9. End-user involvement: Include end-users and other relevant stakeholders in the requirements development process. They possess valuable knowledge about the problem domain and can provide key insights to ensure that the requirements meet your actual needs.

10. Requirements traceability: Establish clear traceability between requirements and other project artifacts, such as use cases,

design documentation, and testing. This helps ensure the integrity of requirements and allows you to track changes and impacts throughout the project lifecycle.

These best practices help ensure that functional requirements are well-defined, understood, and meet end-user expectations.

However, it is important to adapt them to the specific needs and contexts of each project or organization.

Examples.

1. User authentication: The system must allow users to authenticate by providing their credentials (username and password) to access the system.

2. Customer registration: the system must allow users to register new customers, entering information such as name, address, telephone and email.

3. Order processing: The system should allow users to register orders, including information such as selected products, quantity, total amount, and delivery details.

4. Tax calculation: the system must be able to automatically calculate the applicable taxes on the products or services based on specific tax rules.

5. Reporting: The system must allow for reporting, such as a daily sales report, an updated inventory report, or a registered customer report.

6. Inventory management: the system must allow inventory control, recording the available quantity of each product and automatically updating it as sales are made.

7. Integration with payment methods: The system must integrate with payment services, such as credit cards or online payment systems, to process purchase transactions.

8. Email notifications: The system should send automatic email notifications to users, such as order confirmations, status updates, or reminders of required actions.

9. Access control: The system must manage different levels of access for users, ensuring that only authorized users can perform certain functionalities or access sensitive information.

10. Time Reservations: The system should allow users to make time reservations, such as scheduling medical appointments, making restaurant reservations, or booking classes.

Keep in mind that these are just examples, and functional requirements may vary depending on the context and specific needs of each system or project.

5.3   Best practices for non-functional requirements.

Best practices for non-functional requirements are intended to ensure that the non-functional aspects of a system are considered and met appropriately.

Here are some best practices for drafting non-functional requirements:

1. Proper identification and classification: Identify and classify non-functional requirements according to their categories, such as performance, security, usability, reliability, scalability, among others. This helps to better understand the different aspects to be considered.

2. Clear and measurable specification: Write non-functional requirements clearly, objectively, and measurably whenever

possible. Utilize metrics and acceptance criteria to make non-functional requirements more tangible and testable.

3. Defining acceptance criteria: Establish clear criteria for accepting or rejecting non-functional requirements. These criteria should be objective and measurable, allowing for an accurate assessment of compliance with requirements.

4. Validation and verification: Perform validation and verification activities for non-functional requirements. This can include testing, simulations, technical reviews, and audits to ensure that the requirements are correct, complete, and meet expectations.

5. Negotiation and prioritization: Non-functional requirements can have different levels of importance and impact. Therefore, it is important to negotiate and prioritize these requirements according to the needs and constraints of the project. Consider the opinions and expectations of the stakeholders involved.

6. Proper documentation: Document non-functional requirements clearly and thoroughly. Describe the purpose, reason, and acceptance criteria for each non-functional requirement. This helps ensure that everyone has a common understanding of the requirements.

7. Reuse of patterns and practices: Leverage existing patterns and practices for non-functional requirements whenever possible. This can include industry standards, recognized best practices, and established frameworks. Reusing existing knowledge and solutions can save time and effort.

8. Context consideration: Take into account the specific context of the system and the environment in which it will be used. Non-functional requirements can vary depending on the industry, regulation, organizational culture, and other factors. Adapting the requirements to the specific circumstances is essential.

9. Ongoing assessment: Conduct periodic assessments of non-functional requirements to ensure that they are still relevant and meet the evolving needs of the project. Non-functional requirements may need to be updated or refined over time.

10. Effective communication: Clearly communicate non-functional requirements to all relevant stakeholders. Make sure everyone understands the requirements, their implications, and their relationships to functional requirements and other aspects of the project.

Remembering that these are just some of the best practices for non-functional requirements, and it is important to adapt them to the specific context of each project or organization.

Here are some examples of non-functional requirements, which describe quality attributes and constraints on the system, in addition to the functionalities:

1. Performance: The system must be able to process a certain amount of transactions per second to meet peak demands, with response time of less than x seconds.

2. Usability: The user interface should be intuitive and user-friendly, allowing users with different levels of experience to interact with the system efficiently and seamlessly.

3. Security: The system must ensure the protection of sensitive data by implementing authentication, encryption, access control, and other security measures to prevent unauthorized access or privacy breaches.

4. Reliability: The system must be highly reliable, minimizing the occurrence of failures and interruptions. It must be able to recover from failures quickly and maintain data integrity even in adverse situations.

5. Availability: The system must be available for use for a certain period of time, with minimal planned downtime for maintenance and upgrades.

6. Scalability: The system must be able to handle the increased workload and number of users, without significantly degrading performance. It should be horizontally scalable (adding more servers) or vertically (increasing the capacity of existing resources).

7. Portability: the system should be developed in such a way that it is easily adaptable to different platforms, operating systems or execution environments, ensuring its portability and interoperability.

8. Maintainability: the system must be designed in a modular way and with a well-structured architecture, facilitating maintenance, updates, and error correction. The source code must be readable and well documented.

9. Compliance/regulation: The system must meet specific requirements established by relevant laws, regulations, or standards, such as data security, privacy, accessibility, among others.

10. Performance: the system must have an acceptable response time in certain critical activities, such as generating complex reports or performing intensive calculations.

Keep in mind that these are just examples, and non-functional requirements may vary depending on the context and specific needs of each system or project.

6 Business Rules, Validation, and Calculation: Structuring Data Governance with Precision and Consistency

6.1 Business rule.

A business rule is a definition or constraint that governs or guides an organization's behavior, processes, and operations.

It defines how business activities must be carried out, what are the restrictions to be followed and what are the conditions for certain actions to be performed.

Business rules are used to ensure the consistency, quality, and compliance of an organization's operations and processes. They can be expressed in different forms, such as written statements, programming logic, constraints in databases, or automated workflows.

Business rules can cover various areas, such as sales, marketing, production, human resources, finance, and more. They can be specific to an organization, sector, or industry, reflecting the specific practices, regulations, and policies that the company needs to follow.

They are what determine how LLMs should structure reasoning in relation to a given context.

Some characteristics of business rules include:

- Purpose: These are designed to meet a context-specific objective, such as ensuring compliance with regulations, optimizing processes, or improving the quality of products or services.

- Restriction: they impose limitations or restrictions on the actions and activities of the context, defining what is allowed or prohibited.

- Decision logic: they define the conditions or criteria that must be met for a certain action to be performed. These can include validation checks, complex calculations, or specific approvals.

- Evolution: Business rules can evolve over time due to changing context needs, updated regulations, or changes in industry practices. Therefore, they should be reviewed and updated periodically.

- Application: business rules can be implemented throughout the processing chain of an artificial intelligence and in the processes in which data governance is being implemented. They guide the behavior of these systems and processes.

Business rules play a key role in defining and functioning technology product business processes. They help ensure the consistency, compliance, efficiency, and quality of end-product operations and activities.

Here are some examples of business rules in different areas:

- Sales:

    - A purchase can only be made if the customer has a complete and active registration.

    - Special discounts are applied for purchases over a certain amount.

    - A product on sale can only be purchased once per customer.

- Human resources:

    - Employees must comply with a minimum working hours per day.

- The granting of vacation is based on the employee's length of service.

- Promotion to a management position requires the completion of a training program.

- Finance:

  - A customer's credit limit cannot be exceeded.

  - The payment of an invoice must be made within a certain time.

  - The value of a refund cannot be higher than the value of the proven expense.

- Stock:

  - A product in minimum stock should be automatically ordered for replacement.

  - Certain inventory items must be stored under specific temperature or humidity conditions.

  - Perishable products have an expiration date and must be sold before that date.

- Compliance:

    - Certain financial transactions require an additional compliance check before they can be completed.

    - The handling of personal data must comply with privacy and data protection laws.

    - Certain documents and records must be kept for a minimum period of time to comply with specific regulations.

6.2   Validation rule.

A validation rule in a data governance is a rule or condition defined to verify the validity of data entered or modified in the database.

These rules are used to ensure that the data is correct, consistent, and meets the criteria specified by the context.

Here are some examples of common validation rules in information systems:

- Data format: Verify that the data is in a correct format, such as a valid email address, a phone number with the correct structure, or a date in the proper format.

- Value range: Check if the values you enter are within an allowed range, such as a monetary value within a specific range or a quantity that does not exceed an established threshold.

- Data relationships: Verify that related data is consistent with each other, such as verifying that a selected product belongs to a valid category or that a customer has a valid reference ID.

- Mandatory fields: Verify that required fields have been filled out properly, such as ensuring that an address field is not empty or that an ID number is provided.

- Specific business rules: Apply business domain-specific rules, such as checking that a product code is associated with the correct category or that a hotel reservation doesn't conflict with other existing reservations.

- Data duplication: check that the data entered is not duplicated, such as preventing a customer from being registered twice with the same identification number.

- Referential consistency: Verify that references to other data are consistent, such as ensuring that a customer id in a transaction matches an existing customer in the system.

- Data integrity: Verify that data meets established integrity rules, such as primary key constraints or foreign keys in a relational database.

These are just a few of the many validation rules that can be implemented in an information system. The choice and definition of validation rules will depend on the specific requirements and needs of the system and the organization.

6.3   Calculation rule.

A calculation rule in a data governance is a statement or formula that defines how to perform a calculation or mathematical operation based on the data provided. These rules are used to process the data and get desired results within the system.

Here are some examples of calculation rules:

- Financial calculations: Perform finance-related calculations, such as calculating the amount of installments of a loan based on the interest rate, calculating net income based on income and expenses, or calculating the total value of an order considering the discounts applied.

- Data aggregation: Perform calculations to aggregate data, such as adding sales figures by category, averaging a data series, or calculating total items in inventory.

- Unit conversions: Perform unit conversions, such as converting temperature values from celsius to fahrenheit, converting foreign currencies to local currency, or converting units of measurement, such as kilograms to pounds.

- Statistical calculations: Perform statistical calculations for data analysis, such as calculating mean, median, standard deviation, or performing linear regressions.

- Complex mathematical formulas: perform more advanced calculations based on mathematical formulas, such as trigonometric, logarithmic, or exponential calculations.

- Date and time calculations: perform calculations involving dates and times, such as calculating the difference between two dates, calculating age based on date of birth, or calculating time intervals.

- Performance calculations: Perform calculations related to system performance, such as calculating the response time of a transaction, calculating throughput, or calculating the error rate on certain operations.

- Tax and levy calculations: Perform calculations related to taxes and levies, such as calculating the amount of taxes to be paid based on specific tax rates, calculating tax discounts, or calculating the net amount to be received after deductions.

These are just a few of the many calculation rules that can be implemented in an information system. The choice and definition of calculation rules will depend on the specific requirements and needs of the system and organization.

7 Deadline calculation table for auditing data models.

The following table is an example of how you can structure a term calculation to audit data models.

Keep in mind that deadlines can vary depending on the complexity of the model, the scope of the audit, and other project-specific factors.

Activity	Estimated Duration
Data Model Analysis	2 days
Documentation review	1 day
Compliance check	3 days
Test execution	5 days
Analysis of results and report	2 days
Revisions and adjustments	2 days
Contingencies and unforeseen events	2 days
Total	15 days

Table for calculating the deadline for auditing data models.

This table is just an example and can be adjusted according to the needs and specifics of your project.

Additionally, it is important to remember to consider other factors that can influence the timeframe, such as the availability of resources and the complexity of the data model.

8   Example of a data model audit performed on google.

Audit Objective: The audit was conducted for the purpose of assessing the quality, efficiency, and compliance of the data model used by Google in its systems and services.

Scope of Audit: The audit covered the main databases and data storage systems used by Google, with a focus on the analysis and evaluation of the data models implemented.

1. Methodology

Description of the methodology: The audit was conducted following a systematic approach, which involved reviewing the data models, analyzing the structure and organization of the data, verifying compliance with established standards and norms, analyzing the integrity and consistency of the relationships, and evaluating the performance and security of the data model.

2. Audit Results

Audit findings: The following findings were identified during the audit:

• Inconsistencies in the naming and standardization of database objects.

• Failures in normalizing and minimizing redundancies in data models.

• Deficiencies in the implementation of referential integrity constraints.

• Lack of comprehensive and up-to-date documentation of data models.

• Poor performance on complex queries due to indexing issues.

- Potential security vulnerabilities related to the protection of sensitive data.

3. Recommendations

Recommendations for improvement: Based on the findings of the audit, the following recommendations are provided to improve the quality and efficiency of the data models:

- Standardization of naming and naming conventions used in database objects.

- Refactoring of data models to eliminate redundancies and ensure proper normalization.

- Implementation of referential integrity constraints to ensure consistency of relationships.

- Complete and up-to-date documentation of the data models, including description of entities, attributes, and relationships.

- Optimizing queries and improving performance through techniques such as proper indexing and query optimization.

- Strengthening security and protection practices for sensitive data, including regular security audits and review of data access policies.

4. Conclusion

Audit conclusion: Based on the results and recommendations presented, it is essential that Google prioritizes the suggested improvements to ensure the quality, efficiency, and security of its data models.

Implementing the recommendations will result in significant benefits, including greater consistency, improved performance, and increased reliability of google's systems and services.

5. Approval of the Report.

8.1   Data model audit report template.

Here's an example of a basic template for a data model audit report:

- [Company Logo] Data Model Audit Report Date: [Report Date]

- Executive summary: briefly describe the scope of the audit and the main results and conclusions.

- Introduction: Introduce the purpose of the audit and provide an overview of the audited data model.

- Methodology: Describe the approach and methods used in auditing the data model.

- Audit findings: List and describe the findings identified during the audit, including issues, flaws, or areas of improvement found.

- Recommendations: Provide specific recommendations to address audit findings and improve data model quality.

- Conclusion: Summarize the key findings of the audit and reinforce the importance of implementing the recommendations.

Attachments:

- Include any relevant documents or evidence that support the findings and recommendations of the audit.

- Audit Team: List the names and roles of the audit team members.

- Report Approval: Provide space for signatures and report approval dates.

9 Regulatory institutions and auditing of data models in the age of Artificial Intelligence.

Auditing data models is a core process to ensure quality, transparency, and accountability in the implementation of artificial intelligence (AI) systems.

On the global stage, with the increasing adoption of AI in critical industries, the reliability of data models has become a strategic priority.

While there is no single, global institution that exclusively regulates the auditing of data models, a number of international standards, industry bodies, and regional regulators provide specific guidelines that directly impact this practice.

In the international context, the data audit process aims to ensure that AI models are trained and operate on quality data, free of bias and inconsistencies, in addition to complying with the data privacy and security standards in force in the various regions.

Auditing is an essential tool for preserving the integrity of AI systems and ensuring their applicability in an ethical and responsible manner across different industries.

9.1 Global Data Governance Organizations and Standards

At the international level, some global organizations and standards have played a crucial role in defining best practices and guidelines for data auditing, including their application in AI systems.

These organizations do not act as formal regulators, but their frameworks are widely adopted and recognized as a reference by multinational companies and governments.

The frameworks are as follows:

- ISO (International Organization for Standardization). ISO 8000, a data quality standard, and ISO/IEC 38500, focused on IT governance, are two of the main milestones that guide data auditing in AI.

  These standards provide a set of practices that ensure that the data used is accurate, auditable, and ethical.

- IEEE (Institute of Electrical and Electronics Engineers). Through the Global Initiative on Ethics of Autonomous and Intelligent Systems, IEEE works on ethical guidelines that include auditing data, seeking to avoid bias and ensure that AI systems operate in accordance with global ethical principles.

- OECD (Organization for Economic Cooperation and Development). The OECD recommendations on Artificial Intelligence promote an inclusive and ethical approach to AI development, encouraging rigorous auditing of data as a way to ensure accountability and transparency in AI systems.

  This approach has been adopted in several jurisdictions and is a reference for national policies.

9.2   Sectoral and Regional Regulations

In addition to global organizations, various industries and regions have specific regulations that guide the auditing of data models, especially where AI is used for critical decisions.

These regulations are key to ensuring that AI systems operate in accordance with local requirements for privacy, security, and transparency.

1   Financial sector.

In many countries, the financial sector is one of the most regulated when it comes to the use of AI and data auditing. Global financial institutions are subject to regulations that ensure the accuracy and impartiality of AI models used for decisions such as lending, risk assessment, and asset pricing.

On the international scene, we can highlight the following regulators:

- Basel Committee on Banking Supervision (BCBS): The Basel Committee establishes guidelines on the use of risk models, including requirements for auditing data that feeds into these models. The guidelines are followed by central banks around the world and aim to ensure that the data used in AI models is auditable and free of biases that could compromise the integrity of the global financial system.

- European Banking Authority (EBA): The EBA, within the European Union, establishes clear guidelines for the auditing of AI models in the financial sector, including requirements for transparency and accuracy of the data used for automated decisions, in order to protect consumers from discrimination and unfair practices.

2 Healthcare sector.

On the international scene, the healthcare industry is also highly regulated, especially regarding the privacy and security of data used in AI systems.

Data auditing is essential to ensure that the algorithms that assist in diagnoses and treatments are based on accurate and secure information.

- HIPAA (Health Insurance Portability and Accountability Act). In the United States, HIPAA imposes strict requirements on the privacy of health data, and any AI system that uses this data must be audited to ensure compliance. AI models aimed at diagnostics or clinical analysis, for example, need to be audited to ensure that the data used is secure and complies with personal information protection guidelines.

- General Data Protection Regulation (GDPR). In the European Union, the GDPR imposes strict rules on data privacy, which includes mandatory auditing of all systems that use personal data, especially in sensitive areas such as healthcare. The GDPR requires that any AI model that processes personal data be auditable to ensure compliance with individuals' privacy rights.

3   Government sector.

Governments around the world are adopting AI to improve public services, but this also implies the need for rigorous audits to ensure that the data used is accurate and that AI systems are transparent and responsive to ethical guidelines.

- European Commission's Ethics Guidelines for Trustworthy AI. The European Commission's guidelines for trustworthy AI require that all AI systems used by governments be auditable and that data be handled in a transparent manner, with the aim of ensuring that automated decisions are explainable and comply with privacy and security laws.

- Government Accountability Office (GAO). In the United States, the GAO has a crucial role in auditing AI systems used by the federal government. Data auditing is necessary to ensure that AI-based systems, such as those used in public policy and national security, operate transparently and responsively.

9.3   The role of corporate internal policies.

In addition to international and industry regulations, multinational corporations that utilize AI on a large scale need to adopt robust internal policies to ensure auditing of the data that feeds their systems.

Companies such as Google, Amazon, and Microsoft have developed their own AI audit guidelines, often in compliance with global standards, in order to ensure that their models do not suffer from bias and comply with international privacy and security laws.

These internal policies include regular audits of the data used, continuous monitoring systems for detecting inconsistencies, and compliance with the regulations of the various jurisdictions where they operate.

In addition, these companies establish internal ethics committees to evaluate the security and integrity of the data used in their AI models.

10 Data governance and data protection.

Data Protection plays a key role in the context of the institution's data governance, ensuring the transparency, reliability, ethics, and security of the information used and managed by the organization.

Such principles are essential to promote citizen trust, protect privacy, prevent breaches, and ensure that the institution complies with laws and regulations related to data protection.

Corporate Governance involves defining policies, processes, and structures that aim to promote transparency, effective decision-making, and corporate accountability.

In the context of data governance, Corporate Governance establishes the guidelines and mechanisms to ensure the proper and ethical management of data by the institution. This includes defining the responsibilities of managers, creating governance committees, implementing internal controls, and accountability.

Data Protection, in turn, refers to the measures and practices adopted to ensure the confidentiality, integrity, and availability of data, as well as the privacy of citizens' personal information.

The institution must follow the best data protection practices to prevent unauthorized access, misuse, or inappropriate disclosure of data. This includes implementing access controls, encrypting data, conducting security audits, and taking steps to minimize the risk of breaches.

In the context of the institution's data governance, Corporate Governance and Data Protection must work synergistically to ensure data quality, compliance, and protection. Some key practices include:

1   Data governance policies.

The institution must develop clear policies, covering both corporate governance and data protection.

These policies should set out the principles, objectives, and responsibilities related to data management and data protection.

They should reflect the institution's ethical values, ensuring compliance with legal requirements and industry best practices.

2   Organizational structure.

It is important to establish an appropriate organizational structure to implement and maintain data governance and data protection in the institution.

This involves assigning teams responsible for managing, monitoring, and controlling data, as well as implementing clear processes and workflows.

3   Risk assessment and legal compliance.

The institution must carry out risk assessments and ensure legal compliance in relation to data protection.

This involves identifying risks related to data privacy and security, assessing existing vulnerabilities, and implementing risk mitigation measures.

It is also important to keep up with changes in data protection laws and regulations to ensure ongoing compliance.

4   Training and awareness.

The training of the institution's employees is essential to promote data governance and data protection.

Staff should receive regular training on policies, practices, and procedures related to data management and data protection.

In addition, it is important to promote awareness about the importance of data protection and citizens' rights in relation to privacy.

5   Monitoring and continuous improvement.

The institution should establish a regular monitoring system to assess the effectiveness of data governance and data protection. This involves conducting internal audits, analyzing performance metrics, and obtaining feedback from users.

Based on these results, the institution must implement corrective actions and continuous improvements to improve governance and data protection.

11 Conclusion.

Throughout this book, we have explored in depth the key elements that underpin data governance with AI, focusing especially on data model auditing, best practices, and regulations that shape this critical field.

From the beginning, we have emphasized the importance of a well-structured data model as the foundation for any artificial intelligence application, ensuring that data is healthy, free of bias, and ready to feed advanced machine learning systems and LLMs.

We discussed how data sanitation is essential to ensure that models work efficiently and accurately, preventing errors and distortions that could compromise the performance of algorithms.

Additionally, we cover data modeling best practices, including considering functional and non-functional requirements, which are crucial for creating systems that meet both operational needs and regulatory expectations.

One of the most important pillars we detailed was the auditing of data models. We show how it is critical not only to ensure compliance with regulations, but also to provide transparency and accountability in AI systems.

Throughout the chapters, we provide practical examples of how to conduct effective audits, with emphasis on the Google case study, which illustrates the real-world application of these practices in a global technology company.

We also explore how business rules, validation, and calculation are key components for data governance, structuring an environment where AI-based decisions can be made with precision and consistency.

This book has provided the foundation needed to understand how data governance intertwines with the application of AI ethically and effectively.

The tools and methodologies presented aim to help professionals from all areas – data scientists, auditors, IT managers, and compliance consultants – ensure that their AI projects are robust, secure, and in compliance with global best practices.

However, this is just one step in an essential journey in the field of artificial intelligence. This volume is part of a larger collection, "Artificial Intelligence: The Power of Data," which explores, in depth, different aspects of AI and data science.

The other volumes address equally crucial topics, such as the integration of AI systems, predictive analytics, and the use of advanced algorithms for decision-making.

By purchasing and reading the other books in the collection, you will have a holistic and deep view that will allow you not only to optimize data governance, but also to enhance the impact of artificial intelligence on your operations.

With this complete collection, you'll be equipped with the knowledge you need to navigate and lead in the world of AI by harnessing the power of data to turn challenges into opportunities and drive innovations that will define the future of smart technologies.

12 FAQ.

1. What is the main difference between data governance and data management?

Data governance refers to the set of practices, policies, and organizational structures that ensure the quality, security, availability, and proper use of data within an organization.

It defines rules, responsibilities, and processes. Data management, on the other hand, is the operational process of handling data on a day-to-day basis, such as storing, moving, and processing information, being part of daily IT and operations activities.

2. Why is it important to implement data governance?

Data governance is essential for ensuring that data is used efficiently, securely, and ethically.

It helps maintain data quality, compliance with regulations (such as the LGPD), and ensures that the organization has clear control over the use and access to information, as well as improving decision-making based on reliable data.

3. What are the key aspects in implementing data architecture management?

Key aspects include defining a solid governance structure, establishing clear policies on how data is collected, stored, and used, and choosing appropriate technologies and tools to support the architecture.

The integration of different data sources, interoperability between systems, and the standardization of processes are also essential.

4. Who are the key actors in data development?

Key players in data development include data engineers, who are responsible for building and maintaining data pipelines; data scientists, who perform analysis and modeling; business analysts, who identify data requirements; and data stewards, which ensure compliance and data quality throughout its lifecycle.

5. What does the management of operations of a Database Management System (DBMS) involve?

The operations management of a DBMS involves activities such as monitoring database performance, data backup and recovery, access and permissions control, query optimization, and applying security patches.

Ensuring the availability and integrity of stored data is the primary goal of this role.

6. What are the key aspects for managing the operations of a DBMS?

Key aspects include ensuring availability, where systems should be available to users as needed, optimizing performance, to ensure that operations are carried out efficiently, and data security, preventing unauthorized access and privacy breaches.

7. What is the importance of data security management?

Data security is critical to protecting information from unauthorized access, data breaches, and cyberattacks.

Implementing data security management ensures that data is protected at all stages of the lifecycle, and that the organization is compliant with regulations such as the LGPD and GDPR.

8. What are the key players in data security management?

Actors include the Chief Information Security Officer (CISO), who is responsible for information security strategy; system and network administrators, who ensure the implementation of security policies; security auditors, who verify compliance and risks; and data stewards, who ensure data security and integrity.

9. What is master data management (MDM)?

Master data management (MDM) is the process of ensuring that an organization's key data (such as customer, product, and supplier data) is consistent, accurate, and available to all systems and departments.

MDM eliminates redundancies and ensures that a single version of the truth is maintained across the organization.

10. What are the challenges of implementing MDM and RDM?

Key challenges include integrating multiple data sources, maintaining data consistency across different systems, and ensuring teams understand the importance of following master and reference data management (RDM) practices, which include standardized codes and classifications.

11. What is a Data Warehouse and why is it important?

A Data Warehouse is a centralized repository of structured data, designed to store large volumes of information from various sources of an organization, allowing for complex analysis.

It is important because it integrates data from different systems, facilitating analytical reporting, Business Intelligence (BI), and strategic decision-making.

12. Who are the main actors in the management of a Data Warehouse?

Actors include database administrators (DBAs), responsible for the maintenance and security of the Data Warehouse; BI analysts, who extract insights from stored data; data engineers, who maintain data pipelines; and business executives, who define the analytics needs.

13. What does documentation and content management involve?

Documentation and content management involves the storage, organization, and control of documents and unstructured content, such as emails, manuals, contracts, and internal policies.

It is crucial to ensure that all information is accessible, traceable, and up-to-date, serving as the basis for audits and compliance.

14. What are the key aspects of documentation and content management?

The management of documentation and content must ensure accessibility, with all documents properly indexed and cataloged; traceability, to allow audits and history of modifications; and security, with access control and permissions to protect sensitive documents.

15. What is metadata and why is it important?

Metadata is data that describes other data, providing information such as origin, format, structure, and context.

They are essential for data governance, as they help to ensure that data is found and understood correctly, as well as facilitate the organization and efficient use of data.

16. What are the key players in metadata management?

Key players include data stewards, who oversee the quality and consistency of metadata; database administrators, who integrate metadata into systems; and data analysts, who use this metadata to find and understand the data.

17. What is data quality management and why is it necessary?

Data quality management refers to the process of ensuring that data is accurate, complete, consistent, and relevant.

This is necessary for decisions made based on data to be reliable and for the organization to meet regulations and compliance standards.

18. What are the key data quality indicators?

Key indicators include accuracy, which verifies that the data is correct; completeness, ensuring that there is no lack of information; consistency, ensuring that data is uniform across all systems; and timeliness, which ensures that the data is current and relevant.

19. What does the implementation of data governance involve?

Implementing data governance involves creating clear policies and guidelines, defining roles and responsibilities, continuously monitoring data quality, and ensuring regulatory compliance. It is a comprehensive process that involves technology, processes, and people.

20. What is the relationship between data governance and data protection?

Data governance establishes policies and processes for the efficient use of data, while data protection focuses on ensuring the security and privacy of information, particularly personal data.

Together, they ensure that data is used ethically, securely, and in compliance with regulations.

21. What are the main aspects of data protection in governance?

The main aspects include security, which protects data against internal and external threats, privacy, ensuring the ethical use of personal data, and compliance with regulations such as the LGPD, which defines how organizations should treat sensitive information.

22. What is the data audit trail?

The data audit trail is the detailed record of all operations performed on a data system.

It is used to track and monitor activities, ensuring transparency and making it easier to identify problems and fix errors.

23. How is master data used in the context of AI?

In AI, master data is used to ensure that the most important and repeated information (such as customer or product information) is consistent and accurate.

This data is critical for training AI algorithms, ensuring that the system receives reliable and high-quality data.

24. What are functional and non-functional requirements in the context of data governance?

Functional requirements refer to the functionalities and behaviors that the data system must have, such as the ability to process certain operations.

Non-functional requirements, on the other hand, refer to the quality of the system, such as performance, scalability, and security.

25. How does data governance help with LGPD compliance?

Data governance helps implement and monitor practices that ensure the correct use of personal data, including the creation of privacy policies, access control, and anonymization and pseudonymization processes, ensuring that the organization's operations are compliant with the LGPD.

13 Bibliography.

B. SETTLES, Active learning literature survey, Technical Report, University of Wisconsin-Madison D partment of Computer Sciences, 2009.

BERKOVSKY, K. Yu, S. CONWAY, D. TAIB, R., ZHOU, J. and CHEN, F. (2018). Do I trust a machine? Differences in user trust based on system performance, in: Human and Machine Learning, Springer, pp. 245–264.

BERNERS-Lee, T., MANSOUR, E., SAMBRA, A., et al. (2016). A Demonstration of the Solid Platform for Social Web Applications. Published inThe Web Conference. Available at https://dl.acm.org/doi/10.1145/2872518.2890529.

BRETON, Philippe & PROULX, Serge (1989). L'explosion de la communication. La naissance d'une nouvelle idéologie. Paris: La Découverte.

BROWN, C. (2018). Utilizing NoSQL Databases and Big Data Frameworks in AI Projects. Big Data Symposium Proceedings.

CHEN, M., WEI, Z., HUANG, Z., DING, B., & LI, Y. (2020) Simple and deep graph convolutional networks. In ICML.

CRAWFORD, K. Ethics and Transparency in Artificial Intelligence. Research in AI Ethics, 2021.

Data Management Association International (DAMA). (2020). "Data Governance Best Practices for NoSQL Databases and Graphs". DAMA White Paper Series, 7.

DAVENPORT, T. Organizational Culture and Data Governance. Harvard Business Review, 2017.

DAVENPORT, T.H. (2018). The Essential Role of Data Security in Data Governance. Harvard Business Review.

DAVENPORT, T.H., & DYCHE, J. (2013). Big Data in Big Companies. Harvard Business Review, 91(6), 60-68.

FU, Y., PENG, H., SABHARWAL, A., CLARK, P., & KHOT, T. (2022). Complexity-based prompting for multi-step reasoning. arXiv preprint arXiv:2210.00720.

FU, Z., XIANG, T., KODIROV, E., & GONG, S. (2017). Zero-shot learning on semantic class prototype graph. IEEE Transactions on Pattern Analysis and Machine Intelligence, 40(8), 2009–2022.

GEVA, M., KHASHABI, D., SEGAL, E., KHOT, T., ROTH, D., & BERANT, J. (2021). Did Aristotle use a laptop? A question answering benchmark with implicit reasoning strategies. Transactions of the Association for Computational Linguistics, 9, 346–361.

GLIWA, B., MOCHOL, I., BIESEK, M., & WAWER, A. (2019). Samsum corpus: A human-annotated dialogue dataset for abstractive summarization. arXiv preprint arXiv:1911.12237.

GOERTZEL, B. (2014). Artificial general intelligence: concept, state of the art, and future prospects. Journal of Artificial General Intelligence, 5(1), 1.

GUO, B., Zhang, X., WANG, Z., Jiang, M., NIE, J., DING, Y., YUE, J., & Wu, Y. (2023). How close is ChatGPT to human experts? Comparison corpus, evaluation, and detection. ar Xiv preprint arXiv:2301.07597.

HAWKINS, J., & BLAKESLEE, S. (2004). On Intelligence. New York: Times Books.

HELBING, D. (2014). The World after Big Data: What the Digital Revolution Means for Us. Available at: http://papers.ssrn.com/sol3/papers.cfm?abstract_id=2438957.

IMHOFF, C. (2020). Holistic Approach to Data Governance for AI. Boulder BI Brain Trust.

JAJODIA, S., SAMARATI, P., & SUBRAHMANIAN, V. S. (2008). Handbook of Database Security: JAPEC, L., KREUTER, F., BERG, M., BIEMER, P., DECKER, P., LAMPE, C., ... & USHER, A. (2015). Big Data in Survey Research: AAPOR Task Force Report. Public Opinion Quarterly, 79(4), 839-880.

JOHNSON, M. (2018). Data Quality: A Key Factor in Machine.

JONES, A. et al. (2018). "Implementing Data Governance in a NoSQL Graph Database Environment". Proceedings of the International Conference on Data Management, 132-145.

LACITY, M. (2019). Data Governance for AI: Why it's Necessary for Success. Forbes.

LADLEY, J. (2019). Data Governance: How to Design, Deploy, and Sustain an Effective Data Governance Program. Oxford, UK: Elsevier.

LOGAN, D. (2020). The Emergence of the Chief Data Officer. Journal of Data Management, 20(2), 47-52.

LUCKER, J. (2019). Data Governance in the Age of Artificial Intelligence. Deloitte.

O'NEIL, Cathy. (2016). *Weapons of Math Destruction: How Big Data Increases Inequality and Threatens Democracy.* Crown Publishing Group (NY).

OTTO, B., & WEBER, Kristin. (2013). Data governance. In Business & Information Systems Engineering.

REDMAN, R T.C. (2008). Data Governance. Bridgewater, NJ: Technics Publications.

REDMAN, T.C. & SOARES, D. D. (2021). Application of AI in Data Governance. AI Magazine, 37(4), 78-85.

RUSSELL, S., & NORVIG, P. (2009). "Artificial Intelligence: A Modern Approach".

S.A. CAMBO and D. GERGLE, User-Centred Evaluation for Machine Learning, in: Human and Machine

SHIH, P.C. (2018) Beyond Human-in-the-Loop: Empowering End-Users with Transparent Machine Learning, in: Human and Machine Learning, Springer, 2018, pp. 37–54.

SHMUELI, G., & KOPPIUS, O.R. (2011). Predictive Analytics in Information Systems Research. Management Information Systems Quarterly, 35(3), 553-572.

SOARES, S. (2012). Data Governance Tools: Evaluation Criteria, Big Data Governance, and Alignment with Enterprise Data Management. MC Press.

SOARES, S. (2013). Big Data Governance: An Emerging Imperative. MC Press.

TURING, A. (1950). "Computing Machinery and Intelligence". IN: Mind, Volume 59, Number 236, pp. 433-460. Edinburgh: Thomas Nelson & Sons.

WELLS, A., & CHIANG, K. (2016). Data-Driven Leadership. Wiley.

WIECZOREK, M., & MERTENS, P. (2019). Data Governance: A Practical Guide. Englewood Cliffs, NJ: Prentice Hall.

ZHENG, R. and GREENBERG, K. (2018). Effective Design in Human and Machine Learning: A Cognitive Perspective, in: Human and Machine Learning, Springer, pp. 55–74.

"Every great dream begins with a dreamer. Always remember that you have within you the strength, patience, and passion to reach for the stars to change the world."

Harriet Tubman[3]

---

[3] Harriet Tubman (née Araminta Ross; c. 1820 or 1821 – March 10, 1913) was an American abolitionist and political activist. Born into slavery, Tubman escaped and subsequently went on about thirteen missions to rescue approximately seventy enslaved people, including family and friends, using the network of anti-slavery activists and safe houses known as the Underground Railroad. During the American Civil War, she served as a spy for the Union army. After the war, Tubman was an activist in the women's suffrage movement.

14 Artificial Intelligence Collection: the power of data.

The collection, written by Prof. Marcão, offers a deep immersion in the universe of Artificial Intelligence (AI), a technology that is transforming the world irreversibly. In a series of carefully crafted books, the author explores complex concepts in an accessible way, providing the reader with a broad understanding of AI and its impact on modern societies.

The central goal of the collection is to empower the reader to understand what is behind the technology that drives today's world, from its practical applications in everyday life to the ethical and philosophical debates that emerge as AI advances.

Each volume focuses on specific and fundamental aspects of the theme, with explanations based on both academic research and the author's practical experience, making the work indispensable for anyone who wants to navigate this field essential to the future.

14.1 Why study the ARTIFICIAL INTELLIGENCE AND THE POWER OF DATA collection?

We are experiencing an unprecedented technological revolution, where AI plays a central role in sectors such as medicine, entertainment, finance, education, and government.

With a writing that combines clarity and depth, Prof. Marcão's collection makes the topic accessible to both laymen and specialists.

In addition to exploring facts, the work offers reflections on the social, cultural, and ethical impact of AI, encouraging the reader to rethink their relationship with technology.

14.2 Who is the collection suitable for?

The "ARTIFICIAL INTELLIGENCE AND THE POWER OF DATA" collection is aimed at a wide range of readers. Tech professionals will find deep technical insights, while students and the curious will have access to clear and accessible explanations.

Managers, business leaders, and policymakers will also benefit from AI's strategic understanding, which is essential for making informed decisions.

Prof. Marcão offers a complete approach, addressing both technical aspects and the strategic implications of AI in the current scenario.

14.3   The intellectual and practical value of the collection.

More than a series of technical books, this collection is a tool for intellectual transformation. Prof. Marcão invites the reader to reflect on the future of humanity in a world where machines and algorithms are increasingly present in our lives.

15 The books of the Collection.

15.1 Data, information and knowledge.

This book essentially explores the theoretical and practical foundations of Artificial Intelligence, from data collection to its transformation into intelligence.

Focusing on machine learning, AI training, and neural networks, the work is indispensable for professionals and scholars seeking to understand the challenges and opportunities of AI.

15.2 Data into gold: how to turn information into wisdom in the age of AI.

This book looks at the evolution of artificial intelligence from raw data to building artificial wisdom, combining neural networks, deep learning, and knowledge modeling.

With practical examples in healthcare, finance, and education, and addressing ethical and technical challenges, it is ideal for anyone seeking to understand the transformative impact of AI.

15.3 Challenges and limitations of data in AI.

The book offers an in-depth analysis of the role of data in the development of AI exploring topics such as quality, bias, privacy, security, and scalability.

With practical case studies in healthcare, finance, and public safety, it is an essential guide for professionals and researchers seeking to understand how data shapes the future of artificial intelligence.

15.4   Historics are not a thing of the past.

This book explores how data management, especially historical data, is critical to the success of AI projects. It addresses the relevance of ISO standards to ensure quality and safety, in addition to analyzing trends and innovations in data processing.

With a practical approach, it is an indispensable resource for professionals focused on efficient data management in the age of AI.

15.5   Controlled vocabulary.

This comprehensive guide looks at the advantages and challenges of implementing controlled vocabularies in the context of AI and information science.

With a detailed approach, it covers everything from the naming of data elements to the interactions between semantics and cognition. Essential for professionals and researchers looking to optimize data management and the development of AI systems.

15.6   Data Management for AI.

The book presents advanced strategies for transforming raw data into powerful insights, with a focus on meticulous curation and efficient management.

In addition to technical solutions, it addresses ethical and legal issues, empowering the reader to face the complex challenges of information.

Whether you're a manager, data scientist, or AI enthusiast, and for professionals looking to master data management in the digital age.

15.7   Information architecture.

Essential guide for professionals who want to master data management in the digital age, combining theory and practice to create efficient and scalable AI systems.

With insights into modeling, ethical and legal challenges, it is ideal for data scientists, AI engineers, and IT managers looking to turn data into actionable intelligence and gain competitive advantage.

15.8   Fundamentals.

Essential work for those who want to master the key concepts of AI, with an accessible approach and practical examples.

The book explores innovations such as Machine Learning and Natural Language Processing, as well as ethical and legal challenges, and offers a clear view of the impact of AI on various industries, ideal for professionals and technology enthusiasts.

15.9   Large language models – LLMs.

Essential guide to understanding the language model revolution (LLMs) in AI.

The book explores the evolution of GPTs and the latest innovations in human-computer interaction, offering practical insights into their impact on industries such as healthcare, education, and finance. Indispensable for professionals, researchers, and AI enthusiasts.

15.10   Machine learning.

This book is essential for professionals and enthusiasts who want to master revolutionary areas of AI. It offers a comprehensive overview of supervised and unsupervised algorithms, deep neural networks, and federated learning.

With discussions on the ethics and explainability of models, it prepares the reader for the challenges and opportunities of AI in sectors such as healthcare, finance, and public safety.

15.11   Synthetic minds.

A must-read for anyone looking to explore the future of generative AIs, this book reveals how these "synthetic minds" are redefining creativity, work, and human interactions.

Aimed at technology professionals, content creators, and the curious, it offers an in-depth analysis of the challenges and opportunities of these technologies, reflecting on their impact on society.

15.12   The issue of copyright.

This book is a thought-provoking invitation to explore the future of creativity in a world where humans and machines collaborate, addressing questions about authorship, originality, and intellectual property in the age of generative AIs.

Ideal for professionals, creators and innovation enthusiasts, it offers deep reflections and challenges you to rethink the balance between technology and creators' rights.

15.13   Questions and Answers from Basics to Complex – Volumes 1
to 4.

The questions, organized into 4 volumes, are essential practical guides to master the main concepts of AI. The 1121 questions address topics such as Machine Learning, Natural Language Processing and Computer Vision, offering clear and concise answers.

Ideal for professionals, students, and enthusiasts, the book combines didactic explanations with insights into ethics, data privacy, and the challenges of AI, helping to transform your knowledge and explore the potential of this revolutionary technology.

Part 1 includes:

- Information, data and geoprocessing.
- Evolution of artificial intelligence.
- AI milestones.
- Basic concepts and definitions.

Part 2 includes:

- Complex concepts.
- Machine learning.
- Natural language processing.
- Computer vision and robotics.
- Decision algorithms.

Part 3 includes:

- Data privacy.
- Automation of work.
- Large-scale language models - LLMs.

Part 4 includes:

- The role of data in the age of artificial intelligence.
- Fundamentals of artificial intelligence.
- Government, politics and the fight against corruption.
- Mental health.

15.14   Glossary.

With more than a thousand concepts selected from the context of artificial intelligence clearly explained, the book addresses topics such as Machine Learning, Natural Language Processing, Computer Vision and AI Ethics.

Ideal for professionals and the curious, the work offers a comprehensive overview of the impact of AI on society.

- Part 1 contemplates concepts starting with the letters A to D.
- Part 2 contemplates concepts initiated by the letters E to M.
- Part 3 contemplates concepts starting with the letters N to Z.

15.15   Prompt engineering: volumes 1 to 6.

The collection covers all the fundamental themes of prompt engineering, providing a complete professional development.

With a rich variety of prompts for areas such as leadership, digital marketing, and information technology, it offers practical examples to improve clarity, decision-making, and gain valuable insights.

Ideal for professionals, entrepreneurs, and students, this guide reveals how to use the power of prompts to turn ideas into concrete actions and drive impressive results.

The volumes cover the following subjects:

1: deals with the fundamentals. structuring concepts and history of prompt engineering.

2: addresses the Tools and Technologies, State and Context Management, and Ethics and Security.

3: analyzes language models, tokenization, and training methods.

4: It will teach you the techniques to ask correct questions.

5: presents and analyzes case studies and errors.

6: It's your essential guide with the best prompts.

With an extensive collection of practical prompts, the book offers everything from tips for effective communication and decision-making to suggestions for personal development, career, marketing, and information technology.

15.16   Guide to Being a Prompt Engineer – Volumes 1 and 2.

The collection explores the advanced fundamentals and skills required to be a successful prompt engineer, highlighting the benefits, risks, and the critical role this role plays in the development of artificial intelligence.

Volume 1 covers crafting effective prompts, and volume 2 is your guide to understanding and applying the fundamentals of Prompt Engineering.

For those looking to optimize their interactions with AI, the book is a must-have for technology professionals.

15.17   Data governance.

Find out how to implement effective data governance with this comprehensive collection. Offering practical guidance, the books range from data architecture management to protection and quality, providing a complete view for transforming data into strategic assets.

Volume 1 addresses practices and regulations. Volume 2 explores in depth the processes, techniques, and best practices for conducting effective audits on data models. Volume 3 is your definitive guide to deploying data governance with AI.

Ideal for IT specialists, managers, and enthusiasts, it is the definitive resource to ensure compliance, security, and efficiency in data management.

15.18   Algorithm Governance.

This book analyzes the impact of algorithms on society, exploring everything from their foundations to ethical and regulatory issues. It addresses transparency, accountability, and bias, with practical solutions for auditing and monitoring algorithms in sectors such as finance, health, and education.

Ideal for professionals and managers, it offers an ethical and sustainable view of digital governance.

15.19   From IT to AI: the transition guide.

For Information Technology professionals, the transition to AI represents an opportunity to enhance their skills and contribute to the development of innovative solutions that drive the future.

In this book, we explore the reasons for making this transition, the essential skills, a practical roadmap, and the prospects for the future of the IT job market.

Ideal for IT professionals who want to make a career transition to being an artificial intelligence professional.

15.20   Intelligent leadership with AI - transform your team and drive results

This book reveals how artificial intelligence can revolutionize team management and maximize organizational performance.

By combining traditional leadership techniques with AI-powered insights, you'll learn how to optimize processes, make more strategic decisions, and create more efficient and engaged teams.

Aimed at managers, business leaders, consultants, and professionals who want to improve their leadership skills in an increasingly digital world, this book offers practical and accessible strategies for implementing AI in the day-to-day of team management. If you're looking to take your team to the next level, this is the essential guide.

15.21   Impacts and transformations.

The collection covers everything from the technical and ethical challenges of detecting AI-generated text to the influence of algorithms on our digital lives and the transformation of content creation.

The collection also discusses the future of humanity in light of the technological singularity and the dangers of disinformation in the digital age, where artificial intelligence can be used to manipulate public opinion.

- Volume 1: Challenges and Solutions in the Detection of AI-generated texts.
- Volume 2: The Age of Filter Bubbles.
- Volume 3: Content Creation.

- Volume 4: The singularity is near.
- Volume 5: Real Stupidity Versus Artificial Intelligence
- Volume 6: The Age of Stupidity: A Cult of Stupidity.
- Volume 7: Autonomy on the move: the smart vehicle revolution.
- Volume 8: Poiesis and creativity with AI.

Ideal for IT professionals, politicians, academics, urban planners and technology enthusiasts, the collection reveals the social, economic and ethical impacts of this transformation, addressing the reconfiguration of society, cities and the labor market.

"In the information age, knowledge is power, but true wisdom lies in the ability to discern and wisely utilize the vastness of available data."

Brian Herbert[4]

---

[4] American author known for his works in the field of science fiction, especially for having co-written several works set in the universe created by his father, Frank Herbert, in the "Dune" book series.

16 Meet the author. A researcher always in search of knowledge.

I'm Marcus Pinto, known as Prof. Marcão, a specialist in information technology, information architecture and artificial intelligence. With a solid career, I bring you this collection of books, the result of extensive research and study, with the aim of making technical knowledge accessible and applicable.

My experience as a consultant, educator and writer and as an information architecture analyst for more than 40 years allows me to work in strategic areas, offering innovative solutions that meet the growing needs of the technological market.

Over decades, I have developed expertise in data, information, and artificial intelligence, crucial areas for the creation of robust systems that process the immensity of data generated in the contemporary world.

With works available on Amazon, I offer content that addresses topics such as Data Governance, Big Data and Artificial Intelligence, always focused on practical application and strategic vision.

Author of more than 150 books, he studies the impact of artificial intelligence in various fields, from its technical foundations to the ethical implications of its use.

In my lectures and mentorships, I share not only the relevance of AI, but also the challenges and precautions necessary for an ethical and responsible adoption of these technologies.

Technological evolution is inevitable, and my books offer the way for those who wish to not only understand, but master the future. With a focus on education and human development, I invite you to explore this transformative journey through my works.

17 How to contact prof. Marcão.

17.1   For lectures, training and business mentoring.

marcao.tecno@gmail.com

Consulting and Training Company:
https://mvpconsult.com.br

17.2   Prof. Marcão on Linkedin.

https://bit.ly/linkedin_profmarcao